THINK, LEARN & FLOURISH

REDISCOVER YOUR STRENGTH.
REDEFINE YOUR STORY.

NEFFI RAFIYA

BlueRose ONE.com
Stories Matter
NewDelhi • London

BLUEROSE PUBLISHERS
India | U.K.

For permissions requests or inquiries regarding this publication, please contact:

BLUEROSE PUBLISHERS
www.BlueRoseONE.com
info@bluerosepublishers.com
+91 8882 898 898
+4407342408967

ISBN: 978-93-7542-772-8

Cover design: Daksh
Typesetting: Tanya Raj Upadhyay

First Edition: January 2026

Think – Your first step is all about seeing yourself honestly, understanding your patterns, your strengths, your gaps. This is where clarity begins.

Learn – Once you understand, you gather what you need: knowledge, skills, insights, tools, perspective. This is where direction becomes disciplined.

Flourish – Growth, confidence, fulfillment, these don't come from hype. They come from small, steady actions done with intention. That's discipline in its purest form, shaping the life you are meant to live.

In the name of Allah,
the most Gracious and the most Merciful

Acknowledgement

I want to convey my heartfelt gratitude to my husband for his unwavering support and belief in me and my parents for continually being there.

I appreciate the happiness that my siblings and children bring, just by being a part of my life.

I am thankful to Mr. Kabeer Yousuf for his constant support and to Dr. Amrendra Sharma for his guidance and encouragement on this journey.

I also extend my appreciation to my friends and family who took the time to read my book and share their valuable feedback.

A special note of gratitude to Dr. J. Retnakumar, Global Chairman of World Malayalee Federation (WMF), Founder & Chairman of Bhavalaya Art & Culture Foundation, whose support has played a meaningful role in bringing this book to life.

I would not have reached this day without each of you.

Above all, *to the Almighty, without whose will not even a leaf falls*!

Remarks:

"Neffi Rafiya's book on Self-growth is fantastically written, communicating well with the reader, easy to apprehend, and worth pondering over.

It simplifies steps to identify what the obstacles are in front of oneself and how to overcome them with perpetual practice."

-Kabeer Yousuf
Senior Journalist,
Oman Observer Daily

"As Neffi has herself confessed that readers are encouraged to reflect, adapt, or seek guidance based on their unique life journey, ten chapters of the book work as ten important milestones of their life-journey.

Every milestone raises some hope for their bright future and also encourages them to remain grounded in all situations of life."

-Dr. Amrendra Sharma
Associate Professor of English (Retd),
L. N. Mithila University

About the author

Once there was a girl, enthusiastic but not so confident, dreamy yet scared. She believed she had something in her, something that made her special. Maybe it was that heart, which always cared for everyone she loved. Or that mind, which helped her believe she'd figure things out and thrive one day.

Yet, in a crowd, she can be seen in a corner, trying to avoid any gaze directed towards her. She dared not utter a word that might draw attention. She loved living in the background, but in her mind, she was the heroine of the story. Well, everyone is the hero or heroine of their own life, isn't it?

Back in her school days, when people asked her name, she'd say "Neffi Rafiya", hoping they wouldn't ask again. But no, she was always met with a request to repeat it. 'Unique name', 'I never heard that name before', some would say.

"Well, one day, I'll make sure that everyone hears this name", that little mind always thought. She believed she'd write a book and publish it. Her name will be etched on it. She was too young to plan her future, had no idea how to make it happen, but the thought was written deeply somewhere in her mind.

Today, here is my mind working for the input that little girl once gave herself.

Hello everyone, I am Neffi Rafiya, presenting my first book, hoping it helps someone somewhere, to figure things out, love themselves, and live a good life!

"Do not limit your imagination for imagination is the first step of achievement."

Before You Start Reading..

Before we begin, let's sit with some raw truths.

This book is not to fix your life or provide any solution to change anything overnight. And no, I'm not a guru. I don't believe you need one. You don't need someone to "fix" you or walk you step-by-step into self-love. What you need… is to wake up to your own power.

Sometimes, we forget that every answer we're searching for already exists inside us. This book? It's like a mirror that helps you see what's already there.

Let me give you a story. One you might already know in different forms.

There was a man, let's call him Mr A. He was known for his temper and his drinking. His house echoed more with fights than laughter. His two sons grew up in the same home, watching the same scenes. Same chaos. Same trauma. Same father.

Years later, one of them became just like their dad. Hot-tempered. Addicted. Repeating the same patterns. When someone asked him why, he shrugged and said, "What else do you expect? I grew up watching this. That's all I know." But the other son? He turned out completely different. Calm. Disciplined. A loving husband and a gentle father. And when someone asked him why, he answered, "Because I grew up watching this. And I chose not to be the same." Same experience. Two outcomes.

Why?

We don't just grow from what happened to us. We grow through the meaning we attach to those moments. And this book, it's not a manual. It's a reflection of what I've learned along the way. There are no shortcuts here. But if you are ready, there's a path, one that might just help you find your own.

And maybe… just maybe… the right questions that help you see what you've been missing about yourself all along.

So if you're ready, let's walk this together.

Disclaimer:

This book is based on personal reflections, lived experiences, and insights intended for encouragement and self-growth. It is not a substitute for professional advice in areas such as mental health, medicine, or counseling. Each reader is encouraged to reflect, adapt, or seek guidance based on their unique life journey and needs.

Read with an open heart, and take only what truly resonates with you.

Table of Contents

Introduction

The one who has learned to value their peace of mind over society's noisy norms, is also the one who carries a handful of experiences each one whispering that valuing oneself is the greatest wisdom of all.

Who will look after you,

If you refuse to look out for yourself?

Darling, in today's fast-paced world,

Self-love is a must.

Have you ever wondered how much easier life could feel if you truly acknowledged the love you already carry for yourself? Imagine waking up every morning, being in love with who you are, and finding joy in the life you're living right now. That's what self-love is all about. It's about letting go of the comparisons, accepting your flaws, and celebrating your strengths. Like I have mentioned in the beginning, you love no one more than yourself. It's only the matter of honouring it. If you feel like arguing, "But I love my partner, my kids or my parents more", just pause and remember this: that disappointment you feel when your efforts go unnoticed? That's not just a demand for applause, it's your self-love asking you to recognize yourself.

Though no love is greater than the love you hold for yourself, that doesn't mean you love others less, it means the love you offer begins with you, then flows outward.

But let's be honest, honouring that love isn't always easy. From the time we were children, we've all been shaped by what others said about us. Whether it was intentional or not, their opinions crept into our minds and settled there. Over time, those comments became the silent echoes in our head, especially during tough times.

You might have heard about Sigmund Freud, a psychologist who argued this very idea. That, much of our inner dialogues comes from unconscious impressions left in childhood. Even when you are an adult, those old voices resurface, especially during stress.

Have you caught yourself thinking the following phrases?

"Why me?" Does this sound familiar? Do you want more?

"I'm so stupid!"

"Nobody likes me."

"I'm just not creative enough."

"What if I fail?"

"They'll mock me."

Are these the kind of thoughts we should be feeding our minds? No, never. Can you come out of this? Of course, yes. There are many examples in front of you who have successfully got what they wanted out of their life.

Let's dive into a small experiment:

For 7 days, you make it a point to talk negatively about yourself at least once a day to your partner or parents. Let's say the negative trait you focus on is forgetfulness.

Day 1: You casually mention, "I'm so forgetful, I just left my phone downstairs."

Day 2: "I forgot to wear my ring today, I'm always forgetting things!"

Day 3: You start saying, "This is becoming a habit, I forgot to switch off the fan again." Each day, the situation changes, but the message remains the same; you repeatedly reinforce the idea that you're forgetful.

By the end of the week, notice how your family starts responding to you. Perhaps they'll remind you about things more often, almost anticipating that you'll forget something. You've trained them to treat you as someone who is forgetful, without even realizing it. How? The way you spoke about yourself influenced how others saw and treated you.

This experiment shows the impact of self-talk. It's not just about how you treat yourself, but you're also giving others an example of how to treat you. And this is exactly why self-love is so important. When you start practicing self-love and change the narrative about yourself, you are setting a higher standard for how others perceive and interact with you.

Now, imagine flipping that script. What if, instead of calling yourself forgetful, you focused on what you're great at? What if you offered yourself a little kindness, just the way you'd treat someone else you love? That's how you start honouring self-love.

But self-love doesn't mean ignoring your flaws. It means recognizing them, understanding them, and working on them, which is called *self-growth*.

Alfred Adler, another pioneer of psychology, believed that people aren't defined by their past, but by the goals and purpose they set for themselves. He saw growth as the process of moving toward meaning and contribution.

Well, let's stop diving too deeply into the past. Yes, it shaped us. But your brain worked hard to forget some phases and preserve others, for a reason. It did its duty. You don't need to keep reaching the root of every pain to heal it. All you need now is a little understanding, about your thoughts, your patterns, and the truth that many of your beliefs were never yours to begin with, but passed on by others when you were young.

Now that you know it, let's see what Adler said about mental health and healing.

This has been mentioned in one of the blogs on my website, "Adler believed that we can cultivate self-love and resilience by aligning present choices with meaning and belonging." Stop revisiting your pain and giving your brain hints to memorize it again. Instead, shift your focus to what you truly want.

Let us dive a little more into self-growth and see why it matters so much.

Developing a growth mindset:

With a growth mindset, you'll start to believe that your capabilities and intelligence can be improved over time. Studies indicate that individuals who embrace a growth mindset tend to accomplish more compared to those who maintain a fixed mindset. With a fixed mindset, people believe that intelligence and skills will stay the same forever.

It helps you to overcome the fear of discomfort:

I know it is very tempting to stay where it feels safe. Everyone loves staying comfortable, it's easier. I was there too, for a long time. Finding more reasons and excuses to be there. Many more negative self-talk. It takes a lot of effort to incorporate something new in your life when you are too comfortable with how your life is. But if you want to discover your true potential, you'll have to face a little discomfort in the beginning. Self-growth helps you reach your true potential.

Increase your productivity:

Personal growth helps you to achieve focus and a clear vision, thereby increasing your productivity in the workplace. Learning the skills and abilities you need also enables you to accomplish your tasks quicker and easier.

Makes you happier:

Self-growth can make you happier by helping you achieve your goals. You will stop worrying about your flaws and start focusing on becoming the best version of yourself.

Build your self-confidence:

Knowing that you can achieve your goals that you were unable to do previously will boost your self-confidence, which in turn gives you the courage to learn more and achieve more.

Recent studies show that having a sense of purpose is not just motivational. It's scientifically linked to better well-being. Research finds that purpose protects our brain health, supports positive emotions, and lowers the risk of depression and anxiety.

But who cares about all these things when we know life is a ride with ups and downs, right? Well, self-growth isn't about totally changing who you are; it's about becoming the best version of yourself. It's not about having a life without any troubles or issues, but about being the one who can be confident even when life shakes you. Because you know you'll have something or other to worry about and you have prepared yourself for it.

Self-growth looks different for everyone, it also differs according to the stage of life you are in. For some, it's about learning a new skill. For others, it's about breaking free from procrastination, improving emotional intelligence, or simply being kinder to themselves.

And the beauty of self-growth is that it doesn't require big, dramatic changes. It starts with small steps, carefully taken, one at a time. And with each step, you'll notice the changes; in your happiness, your confidence, your relationships, and even your career.

Are you ready to take that first step? Let's walk this path together.

Chapter 1

Find Yourself

"You cannot grow until you meet the real you."

The first step towards your self-growth is knowing yourself and understanding what matters to you the most, recognizing your strengths and weaknesses, and being aware of your thoughts, values, beliefs, and behaviours. You should know who you are. Have you ever tried to do that? Do you know what steps you should take to be happier? Every step you take will impact your life. To understand that better, take a moment and think about yourself in the past. Are you the same person now? Without even a minimal change in your character? That can't be. As we grow up, we'll learn new things, and this will lead to a change in our character. Some call it maturing with age. But it is our experiences and our perspective that help us grow. Yes, your past experiences play an unavoidable role in shaping the person you are. Some people become stronger while overcoming the trauma they face. Some people can lack self-confidence as a result of continuously hearing how incompetent they are from their family or friends since childhood. But what matters the most now is to know what you think about yourself. And you are going to change your life for good soon.

Another part of knowing yourself is to have a deep understanding of your dream and passion. *Who do you like to be when you grow up?* Are you among those who were often asked this question while growing up? It was easy to answer then. As a child, we never had to put much of our thoughts into it. But now, with so many opportunities and so much competition, deciding feels harder than ever. Why is your passion necessary here? Because it is said that you tend to be happier with your job if it is based on your passion, or something you love doing.

Don't just take my words for it. We have Modern motivation research that states, we feel most fulfilled when our work aligns with our inner values and passion. Psychologists Edward Deci and Richard Ryan call this 'intrinsic motivation', and studies show it leads to greater well-being and job satisfaction.

"Get out of your comfort zone!"
"Conquer your fears!"
"Chase your passion!"
Heard it all since childhood,
But never really understood.
All I knew was,
That ain't easy.
And guess what?
I was right.
There are hard days.
Moments of doubt.
Endless questions,
About your choices,
Your path,
Your purpose.
And still,
You keep going.
Because somewhere along the way,
You fall in love
With the joy you feel
Doing what you were meant to do.

So for some people, self-growth might mean finding a career you find interesting or engaging yourself with your hobby.

Now that you know self-growth can be different for everyone, you also understand that it is only you who can figure out what you want from your life. To do that, you need to ask yourself the right questions, or rather right reflections, to understand your needs.

Let's slow down for a while. I'll guide you through some gentle reflections, think of them less as questions and more as doorways. As you write, let your answers flow honestly. This is not a test, it's a conversation with yourself.

Part 1: A Gentle Check-in

Start by writing a small letter to yourself, describing how your life feels right now. Writing could be better, but you can simply think about it if that feels easier. I get it, sometimes lifting a pen feels hard, especially when you worry too much about grammar and details.

Part 2: Zooming In

Now let's assume that your will to try this out wins and you took your pen and paper, and wrote about your thoughts. From that letter, pick three or four areas that stood out for you, it could be health, money, emotions, or something else. For each write, 'what feels good here?' and 'what feels heavy here?'

Part 3: Who You Are At Your Best?

Now write two qualities that help you shine and a time when you used each of them. Some examples are: I am a patient listener; I remember helping a friend through a difficult situation without judging her. I am empathetic; I can easily sense when someone is off and tries to make them seen.

Part 4: The Old Stories

Notice two thoughts that keep holding you back. Write them down, then rewrite each with kinder sentences you'd rather believe. Examples are:

Old thought: I mess things up

Kinder truth: I sometimes make mistakes, but I am learning my lessons and trying my best.

Old thought: I'll never be financially stable

Kinder truth: I am learning to handle money everyday and stability is something that I am building, not what I lack.

Part 5: A Small Next Step

Choose one habit or mindset shift that feels possible this week. Write it as you have already started: *'I am beginning to…'*

What you have just written is a roadmap, a glimpse of where you are and where your heart wants to go. You even know what changes/ improvements you are willing to make. Learning about your interests and then following them can do wonders in your life.

And remember, when you keep postponing a change you've been meaning to make, it often means you aren't fully committed yet. One determined thought can turn that around. Sure, there may be roadblocks or delays, but if you truly mean it, you'll find your way!

Part 6: Let's Play a Mind Game

It's simple and surprisingly revealing. There is only one question. *What are the thoughts that appear in your mind when I say a word?* And I am not going to stop at one word. I will provide you with a series of words. Normally, this game is about instant reaction. You need to answer the one word that pops up in your mind quickly. But here we are reversing that rule. You can feel and understand what your thoughts are, connected with the word I give you. Focus now, take your time, and process your thoughts.

'HOME', ponder over the thoughts that are filling your mind when you think of home?

'FRIEND', let your mind flow with thoughts.

'FAMILY', did you get it now? All these thoughts are telling more and more about yourself.

What next? *'WORK'*, slow down, and think.

'DIET', what are the thoughts you have when you hear these words?

'MONEY', what response comes first?

'HEALTH', well you can add on and process your thoughts more if you wish.

I am concluding the game here. This game has a psychological background; this is Carl Jung's word association test. Your thoughts and feelings that went along with each of the words tell about your current mentality. Your thoughts shape your actions and your actions shape your future. Were your thoughts good enough?

I hope you had many positive thoughts and plans to look forward to. This game really works. Whenever you feel stuck in life, sit for a moment in silence and then try to process your thoughts one after another. If there are many negative thoughts, you know where you need changes. We don't want to go to our future with all those negative thoughts, do we?

Sometimes, people can have negative experiences or thoughts for several areas we talked about above. Does that mean their life is miserable? Well, that's just a phase that will pass. It doesn't need our judgement, but our acceptance, patience and will to bring good changes.

Now that you know more about yourself and your needs, comes the next question. How to achieve it? Well, does it sound weird if I said, I was there too? It took many years for me to figure out what I wanted to do in my life. Once I figured it out, I didn't know what step to take next. Do you want to know what I did to identify my path to success finally? I *started* somewhere. And the path became more straightforward and transparent. That is when I came up with the following lines,

Do you want to seek happiness?

Do you want some changes in your life?

Do you want to be financially independent?

Tell me,

Who is stopping you?

Your fear of starting fresh?

Your fear of failure?

Your fear about what others

might think of you?

In today's world,

where opportunities lie everywhere,

Ask yourself,

What is stopping you?

Yes, some people do fear starting fresh, and some decide that things won't work out for them even before giving it a try.

Don't let your fear conquer you, but learn to conquer your fears.

Let me narrate a short story for you. There was a little boy, Jack, who was just twelve years old. Jack was afraid of thunder and storms. One evening, his mother said it was about to rain, looking at the sky outside. Hearing this, Jack went to his room, shut the door, and slept under the blanket. At the same time, his little sister Jill enjoyed the light breeze, which was followed by drizzling rain. She then found a mesmerizing view of a rainbow up in the sky. For Jill, it was a beautiful experience and a beautiful memory.

Even though this story seems slightly off track, let's make a small comparison. Are you Jack in your life? Letting some fears destroy your beautiful moments. Do you not open the door when opportunities come knocking just because of some fears and negative thoughts? Or are you thinking that your door is invisible because opportunities aren't knocking on it?

The depth of your desire shapes the way you chase it. So now is the time to question yourself once again. Did you wish for anything so intensely that you are ready to conquer your fear and go after it? Or were you just lazy and decided that you were not capable of doing it? Because there is a straightforward step for you to take so that opportunities come knocking at your door. And that simple step is *starting somewhere.* All you need to do is start and the opportunities that once felt invisible will start to appear. Well, this reminds me about one more small but unavoidable topic: *your inner voice.*

The importance of your Inner Voice:

Your inner voice helps you to make quick decisions and makes you feel what is right and what is wrong. It might be already asking you to have self-development. But right when you decide to go for it and try something new in your life, the same inner voice becomes the devil. It might start scaring you. It will tell you everything negative about your new decision. Have you experienced this? Does your inner voice boost your confidence or drain it? If you are experiencing more negativity, it is time to train your inner voice as well. Your inner voice is simply a reflection of what you have fed to your subconscious mind. How do we train inner voices? First, ask what you are feeding to your mind. What do you say to yourself when you are late in doing something? What do you keep blabbering when you are in some trouble? What do you say to yourself when you can't complete the work you started? Your mind is storing each of your negative self-talk. So, instead of letting your inner voice control you, control your inner voice with positive affirmations and self-talk.

No matter how much help you receive,
As much as your plan grows,
You'll have to go through
Uncomfortable and unfamiliar routes.
But, worry not,
Acceptance is the first step.
Growth comes next.
Once you become familiar with failures,
The fear vanishes,
And you become ready to welcome
The challenges that come your way
With arms wide open.
That, exactly, is the sign
That you started flourishing.

Pause & Reflect

- List out three things you've discovered about yourself recently?
- What part of your past shaped the person you are right now?
- What were you doing or who were you with the last time when you were truly happy for being yourself?
- What strengths are you proud of?
- What part of yourself are you ready to accept instead of fix?

SIGNS YOU ARE LYING TO YOURSELF

Let's drop the filters for a moment. Most people aren't confused, lacks potential, or "busy." They're lying to themselves because the truth is uncomfortable. Here are the signs:

1. "I'm confused."

No, you're afraid of choosing. Confusion is safer than commitment. If you don't choose, you don't fail. If you don't fail, no one can judge you. Call it what it is: fear disguised as indecision.

2. "I tried my best."

No. You tried until it became uncomfortable. You're not lacking results; you're lacking skills. And instead of learning, you keep repeating "I did everything." If you really did everything, you would have improved. Skills don't come from intention, they come from grind.

3. "I don't have time."

You have time. You don't have discipline. Two hours on social media is time. Scrolling after dinner is time. Thinking about your dreams instead of working on them is time. You're not out of hours, you're out of priorities.

4. "I'm just unlucky."

Luck isn't your problem, consistency is. You never stay long enough on one path to see results. You change your plan every time it gets difficult. Of course nothing works, you don't work long enough.

5. "My past ruined me."

Your past shaped you, but now you're choosing to stay there. Being an adult means taking the steering wheel, not blaming the road you travelled as a child.

These aren't flaws. These are patterns. And patterns only break when you tell the truth, not the convenient version.

HOW I SABOTAGED MY OWN GROWTH

I want to pretend circumstances slowed me down. They didn't. I did. Here's the truth:

1. I called procrastination "preparation."

I convinced myself that planning, researching, and thinking counted as progress. It didn't. It was fear dressed up as productivity.

2. I chose easy tasks to feel accomplished.

Instead of facing the work that mattered, I picked the work that made me feel good. I wasn't productive, I was hiding.

3. I kept shifting my book's publishing date.

Blaming timing, life, mood, anything. The truth? I avoided the pressure of saying today instead of one day.

4. I over-consumed instead of practicing.

I kept learning, collecting more informations. Not because I needed more knowledge, but because taking action meant I had no excuse if I failed.

5. I changed my goals whenever they became uncomfortable.

Instead of growing, I downgraded my ambition to fit my fear.

6. I blamed circumstances instead of tracking my own habits.

My environment wasn't the problem. My inconsistency was.

7. I waited to "feel ready."

But readiness never came. It didn't even try, until I chose to face my fear.

Self-sabotage isn't dramatic. It's quiet. It looks like waiting, scrolling, switching goals, and calling fear by softer names. And I did all of it.

HOW YOU ARE SABOTAGING YOUR GROWTH

You're not ruining your life with big mistakes. You're ruining it with small, daily betrayals of the person you want to become.

Here's how:

1. You start fast and die out even faster.

Your problem isn't starting. It's staying. You have a burst of excitement, then you disappear the moment consistency becomes boring. This isn't lack of clarity, it's lack of stamina.

2. You reward yourself too early.

One productive morning and suddenly you think you "deserve a break." You treat consistency like an achievement instead of a requirement. Growth needs streaks, not celebrations every two days.

3. You live in reaction mode.

Your mood decides your discipline. Your day decides your plan. Your emotions decide your output. When life pulls the strings, your growth becomes a puppet.

4. You quit the moment progress isn't visible.

If you don't see results fast, you assume nothing is working. But growth doesn't reward impatience, it punishes it.

5. You keep everything in your head instead of on paper.

No tracking. No measuring. No deadlines. No proof of progress. If you don't measure it, your brain will convince you you're doing "enough."

6. You don't build systems, you rely on hope.

You hope you'll wake up motivated. Hope you'll find time. Hope you'll feel productive. Hope is not a plan. It's a slow poison.

7. You only work when the work feels meaningful.

But meaning is rare. Discipline is daily. Waiting for inspiration is sabotage disguised as sensitivity.

8. You attach your identity to your weaknesses.

"I'm not consistent."

"I'm not confident."

"I'm not disciplined."

You repeat these labels until you become loyal to them. That's not honesty, that's self-handicapping.

9. You want the life-changing results without the life-changing habits.

And that gap, between what you want and what you do, that's where every dream quietly dies.

YOUR TURN: IDENTIFYING YOUR SABOTAGE PATTERNS

1. Which pattern from the previous section hit you the hardest, and why?

Write the one you didn't want to admit.

2. What is the one behavior you repeat every day that silently kills your progress?

Be specific. "Procrastinating" is vague.

Name the exact action: scrolling, avoiding calls, overthinking, switching tasks, etc.

3. What is the comfort you keep choosing even though you know it's costing you your growth?

Comfort is the real enemy. Identify it clearly.

4. If someone watched your last 7 days like a movie, what would they say is your biggest form of self-sabotage?

Imagine a brutally honest friend reviewing your week.

5. What do you keep postponing because you're afraid of failing, not because you're busy?

Name the thing you avoid even when you have time.

6. What is the belief about yourself that you use as an excuse to stay small?

"I'm not consistent," "I get overwhelmed," "I'm too sensitive," etc.

Write the belief and the truth behind it.

7. If you removed just one sabotage habit this month, what is the first result that would change in your life?

Describe the difference, clearly and practically.

And hey, if you're curious, you can even ask your ChatGPT to point out the patterns you keep missing, the ones draining you or pushing you to grow. Sure, you shouldn't take it as the ultimate truth (the disclaimer screams that anyway), but sometimes it notices things we overlook. Been there, tried it... still not a fan of replacing human connections with AI, though

You just faced the uncomfortable parts of yourself, the lies, the patterns, the behaviors you didn't want to admit. That was not meant to make you feel guilty. It was meant to make you aware.

Because growth doesn't begin with positivity. It begins with clarity.

Now that you've seen what holds you back, you're finally ready to learn the kind of positivity that's not fake, forced, or borrowed.

Real positivity is built after you face your truth, not before it. So let's move into it with a clear mind, not a comfortable one.

Chapter 2

Learn Positivity

"Your words hold the power you're searching for."

Once you are aware of the negative messages you are sending to your brain and mind, you can begin to change them. Self-awareness and starting self-talk are the keys to gaining control of yourself. It also helps to boost your self-esteem. What is positive affirmation and positive self-talk?

Positive affirmations are simple statements or phrases that you repeat to yourself to change your subconscious thoughts in specific areas of your life. The sentences can be framed according to your needs, or you can refer to several examples. Practising positive affirmations every day encourages you to visualise and believe that statement, which will result in positive changes in your life. "The more you repeat it, the more you believe it."

Psychologists have found that, when your hope and imagination don't align, imagination often wins. Think about that for a moment. If you're hoping for success but constantly imagining failure, your imagination will overpower your hope every single time.

Let's say you're going for a job interview. You hope you'll get it, but if you imagine yourself fumbling and being "not good enough," what message are you feeding your mind? On the other hand, when your purpose is strong, like wanting the job to build a peaceful and secure life, you can train your imagination to see the positive outcome. Silva believed that when purpose is clear, imagination becomes powerful enough to reshape reality. And modern psychology agrees: studies on mental imagery and visualization show that rehearsing success in the mind actually improves confidence and performance in real life.

Psychologists suggest doing positive affirmations every morning with your eyes closed or looking at the mirror. In both cases, you are entirely focused on yourself. You are directing your mind to follow the positive inputs you are giving to it. It is also believed that positive affirmation results in brain stimulation. Repeating the phrases every day encourages you to visualize and accept those statements, which will help you see yourself in a positive light. Some examples of positive affirmations are:

"Today, I woke up feeling grateful and happy."

"I am strong."

"I am confident."

"My past does not define me; my future drives me."

"I am completely focused."

"I am healthier."

"Today will be a productive day."

"I will not let my mistakes define me."

"I have the power to change my mind."

"I am resilient and strong."

"I am stronger than my fears."

And this can go on. You don't need to choose hundreds of affirmations, just a few, depending on your area of improvement.

Anything that you say to yourself can be called self-talk, am I right? In that case, affirmation is also self-talk. Then why am I telling you both the topics separately? Affirmations are intentional, repeated statements designed to shape your mindset, to boost your confidence and know your self-worth.

Self-talk is any running comments and thoughts you have with yourself every day, often without us noticing.

Here, what I am asking you to do is that whenever your inner voice comes with any negative comment, you talk out loud to yourself. You will convert that negative thought into a positive comment. It is not a routine to follow. It doesn't have any fixed time. And you don't need to shout at yourself. I will explain this with an example. Imagine you are going to do something new in your life. Chances are,

1. You are filled with excitement.

2. Your inner voice takes the role of scaring you with negative comments.

You can experience both together. But the negative self-talk has enough power to fade your excitement. So whenever you hear your inner voice saying, *"I cannot do it",* change your self-talk into *"I will give it my best"*. When you think you cannot do something, you are less likely to put effort into doing it. That results in failure, and you will end up thinking, 'I knew I could not do it', and the cycle repeats. But if you are ready to give your best shot, things will be different. Keep doing this without giving in to excuses. Even though this is a simple step, it will be more challenging than you think. We are used to having negative self-talk without even realizing it. And we do this numerous times in our daily life. But keep trying without failure, and you can witness the changes in your attitude. Your day will start to improve as soon as your attitude does.

With that said, let’s pause here for something important. Turning every negative thought into a glowing affirmation doesn't always feel right, and that’s okay. Affirmation can shift your mindset, but they are not meant to feel like lies. If "I am strong" or "I am successful" sounds too far away from your truth, just don't force it. Sometimes, what your mind needs is not positiveness, but neutrality, a gentle space between struggle and positivity. A calm reminder like: 'Maybe, I am not okay now. But it's fine. I won't be stuck here forever'.

When positivity feels fake, it can cause resistance instead of relief. So it's better to start with gentleness by saying things like, "I am trying to understand my emotions", "It's okay if I am feeling low, I'll pause a little and get back later".

You don't have to lie to feel better. You just need to be kind and say what you are ready to believe.

"What if no one bought your book?" my inner voice whispered several times.

"I'd still be happy that it exists in this world," I smiled and replied, always.

Maybe that's what we all need, to accept the doubts, the negativity, but never let them destroy us.

I will give you some examples of negative, neutral and positive self-talk.

"No one likes me."

"I don't feel connected with others right now."

"I like myself."

"I will fail."

"It might not be perfect but let's try anyway."

"I want to succeed."

"I have never done it before."

“It’s unfamiliar, but that doesn't mean I can’t try.”

"It is an opportunity to learn something new."

"There is no way it will work."

“I’ll just give it a try.”

"I can try to make it work."

"I am not going to get any better at this."

“I am still figuring it out.”

"I'll learn as I try."

It is often easy to blame yourself if you messed up something. But once you start practising positive self-talk, it will become a habit. You will stop passing negative comments on yourself with or without knowledge.

Sure, this is a major life-changing step. But do not dream about a massive transformation by following this step for two days or so. Consistency is your best friend here, and with each small effort, you are already growing.

Let me share a bit of my own journey, because I’ve seen firsthand how powerful affirmations can be.

“*I am not chasing fame.*

I am working on myself.

But my work attracts fame.

So I better prepare myself for it.”

This is the affirmation I told myself when I wrote my first eBook. I wasn’t confident back then. I believed I was an introvert, someone who preferred staying invisible in public.

I didn't enjoy being seen, and the thought of attention made me nervous.

Still, I told myself: What if a few people read this book? I should at least be ready to show up.

In the beginning, it was just a mental note to prepare for visibility. But as I repeated this affirmation daily, something shifted. I didn't just prepare, I started believing. I found myself working harder, not to chase fame, but to create something truly valuable for someone out there.

And now look, you're holding that very book in your hands.

That moment taught me something important:

If I could change the way I felt about myself just through a few intentional thoughts, anyone can.

You just need to start talking to yourself with love, belief, and truth, over and over again, until your mind starts to believe it, and your actions rise to match.

Well, there are several other areas to take care of as well.

Preaching values is easy.
Living by them? That's the tough part.
I will not give up.
I won't let anyone treat me like I don't matter.
It's simple to fool yourself with all these words.
But living them out requires strength.
And often, that strength is born from the scars of hurt.
It's okay to get hurt.
It's okay to feel confused.
Life isn't all sunshine and clarity.
The real strength isn't in masking the truth.
It's in accepting it and facing it.

Pause & Reflect

- What is a recurring negative thought you often catch yourself saying?
- How can you reframe that thought into something kind and truthful?
- Which affirmation from this chapter spoke to you the most? Why?
- Write down 3 affirmations that feel personal to you today.
- Would there be a change if you started treating yourself just like how you would treat someone you love?

Chapter 3

Own Your Relationships

"Time with those who remind you of your strength is time well spent."

Remember the story of Jack and Jill? A few days after that incident, one day, Jack was playing with his sister Jill and several other cousins. Jack was feeling proud of himself for looking after the kids so well. He also heard one of his aunts complimenting him, "Jack is such a good big brother". It is then he heard his mother say,

"Once it rains, you will not see him there."

"Is he scared of rain?" Aunt asked, surprised.

"Oh, you should know what happened last time when it rained. He went to his room and slept like a baby while his little sister played all well in the rain," his mother replied.

"And you let her play in the rain?" Aunt was curious.

"Of course, yes. I'll also let Jack join her once he is courageous enough".

Hearing this, a little cousin playing with Jack asked whether he was afraid of rain. Jack explained that he doesn't fear rain but thunderstorms.

Here, Jack was feeling good about himself. He was also happy to hear his aunt notice how good he was. Just then, Jack's mother decided to talk about a past incident. The moment that made Jack feel small. Did she mean to hurt him? No, she was simply sharing a story, unaware of its impact. She also added that she'll let Jack play in the rain once he becomes courageous enough. However, she failed to understand that talking about weakness in front of others is not the right thing to do. Here, so many negative comments entered the little boy's mind. *'He isn't courageous enough', 'his little sister is braver than him', 'he is afraid of the rain'.* If these negative comments were repeated, he'd feed it in his mind. Later, it becomes his belief and self-talk. And you know how having negative self-talk affects one's life. Now, let me narrate this story from another perspective.

One day, Jack was playing with his sister and a few cousins. He was happy. Just then, he heard his aunt complimenting him, "Jack is such a good big brother." He also saw his mother nodding in agreement with a smile on her face. Jack was even happier. The kids joyfully played until the sunset.

Later that night, they returned home. It was about to rain. His mother went to him and started talking to him,

"Did you have a good time?"

"Yes", Jack said happily, yet something was bothering him.

"Are you worried about the rain?" his mother asked. Jack nodded, staring at his feet.

His mother took a pen and a paper. While drawing the water cycle, she explained to Jack how important and a blessing rain is.

"I am not scared of the rain, but the thunderstorms", he said.

"It is like music to the rain. It's okay; you can hold my hand and listen to it. Trust me, we will face your fears together." His mother said, holding his hand.

Now, you decide: which of the above incidents is better for Jack's self-growth? Here, you can take two lessons.

1. To raise your kids well and make them self-dependent by avoiding negative comments.
2. Choosing whom to spend your time with. Who is better? The one who reminds you about your fears or the one who encourages you to conquer them?

Your relationships, whether with your friends, partner, coworkers, or family, don't just shape your emotional health. Decades of study shows that they are the single biggest factor to lead a happy, healthy life, not your bank balance. That is precisely why you should focus on developing fulfilling relationships. A fulfilling relationship is one with trust, respect, and equity, where boundaries are set, and each individual is valued and respected. In a fulfilling relationship, each person feels safe to be themselves and *authentic.*

Surround yourself with positive people who inspire and uplift you to be your best self. The one who understands you, one who encourages you to follow your dreams and ideas, supports your growth and celebrates your success.

To achieve such a fulfilling relationship, you'll have to take some steps initially. Be honest. Yes, the one who is with you should know the person you are. Be frank about your likes, dislikes, passion, and hard work and how much you would appreciate their support. Notice even the tiny things that your family, friends, or colleagues do for you, and be grateful for them. Let them know your appreciation. Practising gratitude not only makes them happy but also helps you to focus on the bright side. Studies show that expressing gratitude strengthens relationships. Couples who regularly thanked each other reported greater satisfaction, and even workplace studies found that gratitude boosts trust and cooperation.

Now, these are several steps you can take to let those around you know about your welcoming and loving nature. Remember, you are not accountable for everyone's character but yours. Be wise and filter the comments you receive. Decide what to let your mind accept and what not to. Also, set healthy and positive boundaries wherever you feel necessary.

Self-love, self-growth, keeping boundaries, all of these are necessary, no doubt. But sometimes, selfishness disguises itself as self-love. That's when you start believing you shouldn't adjust, not even a little, for anyone's sake. Well… that's where we go wrong.

No two human beings are built the same. Their emotional intelligence, perception, and reactions differ. What feels right to you might feel wrong to them, and that's okay. When you feel the need to draw strict boundaries with the people you love (and yes, sometimes you should), make sure you aren't building walls so high that love can't climb over.

Because if you're not willing to compromise at all, even for those who matter, in the name of your happiness, it's time to pause and reflect. Human beings need connection. And connections require a little give and take.

Running away from such moments or keeping too rigid a boundary doesn't make you strong, it just makes you lonely. And loneliness was never the aim of self-love.

Even if you try to be the best version of yourself, some people will still hurt you, and never even realize they did. They won't apologize. They won't see their mistake. And the more you chase their understanding, the more chances you give them to break you again. So sometimes, you gotta learn to protect your peace and live your life.

How peaceful it feels

to realize your worth

And stop chasing the why's

That never brought closure anyway.

Sometimes, you might need more inspiration and guidance to reach your goal, even if you know what your dreams and interests are. Sometimes, you might also need someone to help you figure out what you want to do in your life. This is where the right mentor or the right personal coach plays a role. Just imagine how much you would progress when someone who is non-critical and understanding is there on your side. The one who is ready to hear your problems. Someone who understands about focus, goals, and how to stay motivated. The one who would ask you the right questions and help you discover the correct area of focus in your life. That is how having a mentor or personal coach helps you out. If I simplify further, there are two paths to achieve self-growth. One where you have the help of a personal mentor or coach to guide you in the right direction. This path is often easier. The other one is where you discover everything about you by yourself. And that might be a bit complicated. You might have to go through some failures to understand what works for you finally. You might have to face some stressful days. You might have to do more research and work hard to reach your goal. But once you set your mind, trust me, you will achieve it, and everything will be worthwhile. Now you can decide which path to choose.

A Simple Truth About Mentorship

Do you want a roadmap to success, or are you ready to forge your own path?

People often ask if there's a shortcut, a cheat code, to success. Honestly, I'm not sure if there is. What I've learned through experience is that growth comes when you keep showing up, learning, failing, and trying again.

I've come across many webinars and "gurus" promising, "Follow my roadmap, and you'll be successful."

But let's pause and think, if someone else has already faced all the challenges, learned the lessons, and then handed you a shortcut, what do you really gain?

Maybe quick results, like increased sales, or visibility. But not the wisdom that comes from walking the path yourself.

That's why I believe in slow learning, one concept at a time, one effort at a time. When I mentor women who are just starting their writing journey, I remind them that the process is the growth.

There's no rush.

There's no perfect formula.

Because the lessons we learn while struggling, adapting, and standing back up again, those are the ones that shape not just our success, but our strength.

And there is one more thing to care about: be bold about seeking feedback. You are growing. You are flourishing. Getting some feedback will help you know whether your direction is right. It will help you to boost your confidence and correct your mistakes. Asking for feedback will give you another viewpoint to improve yourself. You need to make sure that you approached the right person to get the feedback. That can be your friends, coworkers, or anyone among the family, whoever you trust. The one who truly sees your growth, not just your flaws.

Ready for a hard truth break?

A truth about human nature is,
we often forget to live in the present,
chasing a beautiful future
We're trying so hard to build.
And you expect those people
to care about you?
Snap back to reality.
Only a few around you
truly deserve your time,
your trust,
your heart.

Pause & Reflect

- Does anyone make you feel safe, seen, and supported?
- Are there relationships in your life that make you shrink or stay silent?
- What does a fulfilling connection look like for you?
- Are there boundaries you need to express more clearly?
- Who do you need to appreciate out loud today?

Chapter 4

Reinvest in Yourself

"You are your life's most important project. Pour into yourself, without guilt."

Another significant step towards self-growth is investing in yourself. Yes, investing in yourself boosts your well-being, expands your knowledge, and improves your overall productivity and happiness.

There are several parts to talk about investing in yourself. First, let us talk about investing some *time*.

If we are talking about taking care of oneself, there are a lot of things that you should give to yourself. Respect, love, rest and the list goes on. One precious gift among them is time. Benjamin Franklin's quote, '*Lost time is never found again,*' emphasizes the importance of time.

I will divide investing time into three categories.

Adequate resting hours

Picture yourself having a moment of relaxation with a cup of tea. Doesn't that sound good? We all love taking some rest. But are you getting all the rest you need? I will list it down for you.

1. Physical rest: This includes active and passive rest. Good quality sleep comes under passive rest, which is very essential. While active rest includes lying down, stretching or relaxing your muscles, and meditation.
2. Mental rest: A break from mentally demanding work. Recharge your mind and body by connecting with nature because nature can do wonders.
3. Sensory rest: a much needed pause from all the noise and stimulation around us. When you find yourself thinking that everyone else is living a meaningful, happy life while you're stuck in an unfair season, remember, no life is perfect. It's just social media

overfeeding you polished snapshots that create a false picture of perfection. Stepping away from screens, bright lights, and constant noise by choosing a dimmer, quieter space eases the strain on your senses. And when your senses rest, your mind finally gets the chance to feel calmer, lighter, and more focused.

4. Emotional rest: It means to feel and express your emotions healthily.
5. Creative rest: When you rest creatively, you give your mind time to explore new ideas. This will boost your inspiration and help you to be motivated. Engage in some creative activities like drawing, knitting, or anything that you enjoy.
6. Social rest: Taking a break from social interactions that we face every day. It means spending some time with your loved ones and having a 'me time' doing something that you love.
7. Spiritual rest can include gratitude, prayer, and volunteering for a cause that you care about.

> A quiet reminder: If you feel like you have no one to talk to, just remember, He's always there. And even your whispers will not go unnoticed.

Now, before you feel overwhelmed about all these rests..

Yes, there are seven types of rest, and each offers its own kind of nourishment. But let's be honest: trying to 'do it all' isn't realistic, especially every single day. Life can be messy. Time is limited. And some days, even taking a breath feels like a win, and that's okay too.

The goal here is not to create a checklist that stresses you out even more. It is all about awareness. Knowing the kind of rest your body is craving for, right now.

Maybe, today, it's about a few minutes of reading or simply giving yourself permission to do nothing for a moment without any guilt.

Rest is not about perfect harmony. It's about the presence of your mind.

Reading

You've probably heard this a hundred times, reading is a good habit and it truly is. Reading is a great way to promote self-growth. If you've pinpointed the areas where you'd like to improve, reading can be an excellent tool to help you forward. You can easily find a book or an article related to your chosen topic. However, don't limit your reading to such books. You may learn something new with fiction or nonfiction books as well. Books serve as an excellent source of knowledge and inspiration.

Journaling

Writing a journal has essential benefits for personal growth. It helps reduce stress and anxiety while supporting your mental well-being. You can gain self-awareness by writing down your thoughts, behaviours, and activities. It also enables you to identify your behavioural pattern.

If you are experiencing any problems, writing them down can help you find solutions because you may start seeing things differently once you have written them down. Journaling also serves as an emotional release since you're sharing your feelings in a safe, judgment-free space.

Then comes the second part of the investment. Investing your energy. You can be very productive and energetic only if you are physically and mentally healthy. Following certain habits such as staying hydrated, eating nutritious food, and being physically active also have critical roles in reducing the feeling of tiredness.

Your body does communicate with you. Listen to it, understand it, and make the necessary changes to improve your overall health, if needed.

Now, you know the area to focus on for your improvement and how to spend your time and energy productively and thereby attain good results. And yet, there is one more investment, which is often the biggest reason people hesitate or procrastinate. Investing your money. The main reason why you have to invest your money for self-growth can be *to learn*. Remember, successful people always continue learning. We will discuss this investment in detail in the next chapter.

A Gentle Flourish Practice:

You know the breathing exercise they all talk about, "*one hand on your chest, the other hand on your stomach ..now breathe in through your nose and out through your mouth*". Well, the hands are placed to track the movements, Feel your stomach rise as you inhale deeply, and your chest stays still. This is called diaphragmatic breathing, a simple yet powerful way that strengthens your diaphragm, increases the lung capacity and improves oxygen in take. Higher level of oxygen enhance energy, focus, and emotional balance, helping you feel calmer, more confident, and connected to your body.

Pause & Reflect

- In what ways have you neglected yourself lately, mentally, emotionally, or physically?
- What does “rest” truly mean for you?
- Which kind of rest do you need the most right now: physical, mental, emotional, creative, spiritual, or social?
- List 3 ways you can invest in yourself this week (even if they’re small).
- How do you feel when you treat yourself like you matter?

Chapter 5

Improve Skills

"Your mind was made to bloom.
Keep watering it."

If *being more confident about yourself* is something you want to achieve, you should not skip this step. There is, perhaps, no greater investment than learning new skills. It can be learning a new language, time management, or honing your technical abilities. Today, gaining a new skill or pursuing further education is just one click away. Be honest, how many times have you come across courses, online or offline, and just scrolled past them?

I am not asking you to go and learn everything that is available. No. But once you figure out your passion or interest, start investing your time, energy, and money to attain more knowledge about it. Because the process of learning not only expands your knowledge base but also helps you achieve a mindset of continuous growth and development. You can also make use of the smartphone and the internet to gain knowledge. You can read articles about it or watch a video on YouTube. You know it already. *When in doubt, Google it.* Isn't this how we find answers these days, being resourceful? It is good unless and until you start googling about your diseases. No sir, you need to visit your doctor about that.

Investing in yourself through learning new skills has a lot of benefits. Let us talk, in detail, about how this commitment to self-growth can transform your life and career.

Learning new skills helps to increase your knowledge and understanding in many areas. It opens up a whole new world of information and opportunities before you. Each new skill you learn acts like a new tool added to your tool kit. It empowers you to face your challenges with confidence and creativity. Learning new skills, therefore, enables you to open the doors to many opportunities that were previously shut. Each skill you learn brings you one step closer to the version of yourself you're meant to become.

Look around you. Look at the world you live in. Is it the same as ten years ago? Think about it. The world is rapidly evolving. Staying relevant and competitive requires the ability to adapt and continually acquire new knowledge. Investing in yourself through skill development is a form of lifelong learning. It is also better if you keep updating your skills. Let us go through an example. Once, there was a time when writers used typewriters. Then came the computer. Now, we are using laptops and smartphones. The skill remained, but the technologies have evolved.

By nurturing a mindset of lifelong learning, you position yourself as an active participant in your own growth and development journey.

Learning new skills can also be a game-changer in career advancement. Employers value candidates who demonstrate an openness to learning and growing. Imagine yourself as an employer. Wouldn't you value employees who are committed to professional development? Whether you're employed, freelancing, or running your own business, constantly learning helps you stand out.

Whether you are aiming for a promotion within your current job or seeking new opportunities elsewhere, adding new skills can set you apart from the competition. Staying up to date with technological progress is necessary. Otherwise, you may find it hard to achieve your career goals.

But it's not just about career or success. Learning new skills also brings personal fulfillment and well-being. Engaging in activities that challenge and stimulate your mind enhances cognitive function. It also gives you a feeling of satisfaction and achievement. It helps uncover parts of yourself you didn't even know existed. Whether you're exploring a new hobby or a subject of personal interest, the process of learning itself can be advantageous.

Learning new skills requires dedication, perseverance, and resilience. These qualities are extremely useful in facing the challenges of life. By stepping outside your comfort zone and embracing the learning process, you acquire the resilience needed to overcome obstacles. *Each new skill mastered is evidence of your ability to adapt and grow, handling adversity.*

Remember, the journey of self-growth begins with a small step. Start investing in yourself. Start educating that beautiful mind of yours and watch as each new skill is acquired, unlocking your full potential to shine in this rapidly changing world.

Pause & Reflect

- What is one skill you've always wanted to learn but kept postponing?
- What's holding you back from starting?
- What tiny step could you take today to move closer to learning it?
- How do you feel when you master something new?
- What skill or strength do others often notice in you that you may not fully recognize in yourself?

Chapter 6

Stay Consistent

"Keep showing up,

Even when it's hard.

Especially when it's hard."

Self-growth. We love how it sounds, don't we? It looks beautiful on vision boards, inspiring in Instagram captions, and magical when you read about it in books. But living it? That's a whole different story.

The truth is, self-growth is messy. It's full of late night doubts, and moments when you just want to say, "Forget it. I'm done." It's the kind of journey that tests your patience, your discipline, and your ability to fight that little voice in your head that whispers:

"Just skip it today. You can do it tomorrow."

That voice? That's procrastination. And let's be real, we've all given in to it at some point.

Why do we procrastinate?

It's not because you're lazy. In fact, most people who procrastinate aren't lazy at all, they're overwhelmed. Big goals look scary. The thought of doing something hard triggers discomfort, and our brain hates discomfort. So, what does it do? It looks for an easy escape.

Scrolling social media? Easy. Watching Netflix? Easy. Rearranging your wardrobe instead of writing that business proposal? Weirdly easy too. Why? Because these activities give you instant gratification, tiny hits of dopamine that feel good right now.

But here's the problem: those small escapes cost you big in the long run. They steal the time you need for the things that truly matter.

If you've ever found yourself saying, "I'll start tomorrow," just know, you're not alone. But also know this: you can break the cycle.

So, how do you stop procrastination from winning? The secret is simple, but not easy: start small and stay consistent.

When you look at your big goal, whether it's writing a book, building a business, losing weight, or running a marathon, it feels huge, doesn't it? Overwhelming even. That's why you need to break it down.

Think of it like this: you wouldn't swallow a whole pizza in one bite (well, hopefully not). You eat it slice by slice. Your goals work the same way, tiny steps, one at a time.

Here's a powerful approach:

Set a clear, specific goal. Not "I want to get fit," but "I want to run a marathon in six months."

Break it into sub-goals. Weekly targets. Daily actions. Things that feel doable, not scary.

Sounds simple, right? But let me show you why it works with Tom's story.

Tom had always admired marathon runners. Their determination, their discipline, the sheer strength of crossing that finish line, it inspired him. So one day, he said to himself: "I'm going to run a marathon."

The excitement was real… for about a week. Then reality hit. 42 kilometers? How on earth am I going to do that? Suddenly, his dream felt like a nightmare. Training looked impossible. He started making excuses:

"I'm too tired today."

"Work is crazy right now."

"I'll start on Monday." (By the way, that particular Monday never comes.)

Sound familiar? That's procrastination's favorite game, convincing you that later is better. But Tom had a choice, just like we all have it: keep delaying, or start small. He chose the second option.

Instead of obsessing over 42 km, he set a tiny goal: three runs a week. Short distances at first. He didn't care about speed or stamina, just showing up. And guess what? He did it.

That small win gave him confidence. Then he added another goal: improve his pace. Later: incorporate strength training. Then: sign up for shorter races.

Every little milestone became fuel for the next. Did he face setbacks? Absolutely. He got injured. He had bad days. He even skipped a few runs. But he didn't quit, because he had a system, not just a dream.

Months later, Tom crossed that marathon finish line. And in that moment, all the small steps, all the boring days, all the struggles, every bit of it was worth it.

Here's what Tom's story teaches us:

- Big goals are built on small, consistent steps.
- Procrastination dies when progress feels possible.
- Persistence is more powerful than motivation.

The Power of Consistency

Let me tell you a secret: success doesn't come from doing big things once in a while. It comes from doing small things consistently, even when no one is watching, even when you don't feel like it.

Progress isn't loud. It's quiet, almost invisible in the beginning. But over time, those tiny efforts compound. They turn into habits, and those habits shape your life.

And here's something no one talks about: consistency feels hardest when life feels… silent. Think about it. When something exciting is happening, a job interview, an important meeting, a big celebration, you're buzzing with energy. The highs feel good. Even the lows, like sadness or challenges, give you something to overcome. That's what makes life colorful: the ups and downs, the drama, the rush.

So what makes life boring? Not the bad days. The idle ones. The days when nothing happens. When you stop trying. When you let the silence stretch until it feels like nothing matters.

That's why consistency is so powerful. In those quiet seasons, the ones with no noise, no thrill, no urgency, your choices matter most. You can wait for life to hand you excitement, or you can create your own momentum. You can decide to grow, even when it's not glamorous.

Because real change doesn't happen in the highs or the lows. It happens in the stillness, when you choose action over comfort, when you refuse to give up just because it's boring.

So, when you feel like giving up, remember this:

- You don't need to be perfect. You just need to keep going.
- Small steps today create big wins tomorrow.
- Every time you choose progress over procrastination, you're building strength.

Self-growth isn't a straight road. There will be potholes, roadblocks, and days you'll feel like turning back. You'll question your decisions. You'll wonder if it's even worth it. Those are the moments that matter most. Why? Because that's where your resilience is born.

When procrastination whispers, "Take it easy," answer back: "Not today." When doubt says, "You can't do this," remind yourself: "Watch me."

Your journey won't be easy, but it will be worth it. Every small step counts. Every time you push through resistance, you're not just moving closer to your goal, you're becoming stronger, wiser, and more unstoppable than ever before. So no matter how long it takes, no matter how many times you stumble, remember this: never give up.

Before you go further, let's pause a little to understand how our mind works.

Our minds are restless, always wandering between the past and the future. They replay what's already done and worry about what's yet to come.

After an argument, you might think of the perfect thing you could have said. In the shower, your thoughts may jump from old mistakes to all the things you still need to prepare for. And soon, your body feels what your mind thinks, stress takes its toll. So, how can you take back control?

Start by being mindful, as much as you can. When your mind drags you into the past, pause and recognize what's happening. Remind yourself, "Ah, my mind is playing its game again." You can choose not to play along, and the thought will fade.

If anxiety about the future creeps in, do the same. Remember: outcomes are not always the result of your efforts alone. Your role is to do your best, not to judge yourself for what follows.

When your thoughts start racing and you catch yourself midstream, wait. Stay still. Watch your next thought arrive. You'll notice how your awareness takes the mind off guard.

Stress, regret, and anxiety aren't always enemies. In moderation, they're teachers, showing you what to avoid, prepare for, or understand better. Use them wisely, but never give them the power to destroy you.

Be mindful and stay present.

Pause & Reflect

- When was the last time you pushed through something difficult? How did it feel afterward?
- What goal have you given up on that still tugs at your heart?
- What would it look like to try again, just a little?
- What's one thing you've learned from a setback in your life?
- What keeps you going when things get tough?

A pressure that works

You know why you submit your college assignments on time? Not because you're disciplined. Not because you love the subject. But because there's a date.

You don't negotiate with that deadline. You don't wait for motivation. You don't care whether you're tired or inspired. You just do it, because there's no choice left.

That's the power of a date.

And sure, back then we still found shortcuts. We copied our friend's assignment at the last minute. We laughed through the panic, handed in the same answers, and the professor simply said,

"I only need to check one. Yours are identical anyway."

That was a life where mistakes were negotiable. Where someone always had a quick fix. Where effort could be borrowed.

But adulthood hits differently. Your friend can't hand you their progress. Your colleague can't lend you their growth.

There's no assignment to copy, unless you count copying people's lives on social media, which still gets you nowhere.

People don't lack potential. They lack consequences.

Set a deadline that forces you to move, a day that doesn't care about your excuses, your moods, or your "I'll start tomorrow." Because the truth is simple: without a deadline, you'll keep treating your dreams like suggestions.

Back then, when I still had "circumstances" to blame for delaying my book, I picked December 2025 as my deadline.

And by mid-November, everything suddenly started falling into place.

Nothing in my life changed. No new pressure. No external push. The only thing that shifted was this: my mind refused to cross that deadline without at least trying.

That's the power of a date, it corners you until effort becomes non-negotiable.

Chapter 7

Honor Your Wins

"The difference between making your progress a pressure or a purpose lies in celebrating every win."

Celebrating success is just as crucial as persisting through challenges. It's a way to acknowledge your progress, strengthen your positive habits, and cultivate a growth mindset. Every milestone you reach, no matter how small, has the potential to be life-changing if you choose to celebrate it.

Why celebrate success, you may ask? Well, celebrating your achievements, big or small, is a powerful way to reinforce positive habits and boost your sense of accomplishment. It reminds you of your capabilities and motivates you to continue pushing forward, even when faced with adversity. Additionally, celebrating success will help you cultivate a growth mindset by shifting your focus from fixed outcomes to the process of continuous improvement.

Embracing change is an essential part of personal growth, and celebrating success plays a vital role in this process. When you celebrate your achievements, you become more open to growth and new opportunities. It promotes the idea that change is not something to be feared but is to be accepted as a tool for growth and transformation.

Celebrating doesn't always have to be reserved for huge accomplishments. Recognizing and acknowledging your small achievements along the way is equally important. These small wins not only provide a sense of satisfaction and motivation but also serve as building blocks for more significant achievements. But it isn't about rewarding yourself for doing the bare minimum, it's about honouring progress that moves you forward. And no, celebration doesn't always mean throwing a party or posting on instagram. Sometimes, it's as simple as whispering to yourself, "I am so proud of you". Here are some ideas to celebrate success in meaningful ways:

Acknowledge Your Achievements: Take a moment to reflect on your progress and acknowledge the hard work and effort you've put into reaching your goals. Write down your achievements in a journal or share them with a friend or a loved one.

Treat Yourself: Give yourself a little treat as a reward for your hard work. Whether it's something simple, like your favourite meal or a quiet, relaxing day, give yourself permission to enjoy it.

Share Your Success: Celebrate your achievements with others by sharing your success story. Whether you post on social media, write a blog post, or give a presentation, sharing your accomplishments can inspire others and reinforce your sense of achievement.

Set New Goals: Let your success become a springboard not to pressure yourself, but to keep growing with joy. Celebrate each new milestone along the way and keep pushing yourself to reach new heights.

Express Gratitude: Take the time to express gratitude for the support and encouragement you've received from others along your journey. Whether it's sending a thank-you note or simply saying "thank you," expressing gratitude can deepen your sense of connection and appreciation.

You've come so far, don't forget to look back and smile before you look ahead. Life isn't just about stacking achievements. It's about living it fully.

As you reflect on all your small and big wins, I want you to remember something that might surprise you.

Sometimes, I used to imagine my life as a movie,

And myself as the lead character.

No matter what life threw my way,

The main character would always win.

I believed everyone should think like that,

To feel their self-worth,

And live with a little more peace.

Yes, no one but you matters the most.

But isn't it funny?

Many "main characters"

Who once walked this very ground,

Are no more.

It's a grounding thought, isn't it? This isn't meant to scare you, but remind you. While you're dreaming big and becoming better, don't forget, nothing lasts forever. Chase your goals. Try harder. But don't lose yourself, or the people who truly love you, along the way.

You weren't born to impress the world. You were born to know yourself. To live truthfully. To exit this ground gracefully, with your heart full and your soul at peace. Achieve what you once dreamed of, not for applause, not for validation, but for the quiet satisfaction of telling yourself:

"I did it. And I did it my way."

Because this life, this fleeting little span we're gifted on Earth, use it to be unapologetically, fearlessly, audaciously You.

Pause & Reflect

- What is one win you haven't celebrated yet? Pause and honour it now.
- What's a recent moment where you felt proud of yourself?
- How do you usually celebrate your own efforts? Could that change?
- Who do you want to share your success with, and why?
- What does "enough" look like for you today?

Before You Close This Book...

"Transformation happens in every small decision to keep going."

It all begins with knowing yourself. That's the foundation for personal development. Positive affirmations and self-talk then empower you to face challenges with clarity and build a resilient mindset. Developing fulfilling relationships nurtures support and connection. Investing in yourself is crucial for growth, whether through education, experiences, or self-care practices. Learning new skills keeps your mind sharp and opens doors to new opportunities. And when the journey feels tough, perseverance becomes your quiet power, never give up, even when faced with obstacles or setbacks. And finally, celebrate every success, no matter how small, as each achievement reflects the strength it took to get there.

Together, these seven steps form a gentle roadmap, one that helps you keep growing, glowing and becoming. Walk through each step with determination and mindfulness, and watch as you transform into the best version of yourself.

Remember, you already have the power to shape the life you desire. So walk forward with belief. Shine bright. And never forget:

Your adventure of self-discovery awaits!

Now that you have learned to grow, remember to rest too, to take your time before starting the next chapter of your life.

Slow down,

You don't need to glow today.

You can just walk astray,

Letting the darkness swallow you, Not in despair,

but in acceptance.

Let it make you fall.

You don't need to fight or strive.

You are allowed to just exist, To crumble, to yawn,

To let the world blur a little.

Sometimes, that's what healing looks like,

Lying still,

And doing nothing brave.

But deep down, believing

That you'll come back with grace,

For no one else, but yourself.

Sure, the lotus blooms in mud.

But that doesn't mean,

You have to stay in the dirt.

You could be a Jasmine,

Or a wide sunflower.

Who knows what you are meant to flourish into.

Bonus Chapter

Stay True, Stay You

"Authenticity is not selfish. It's the foundation of love that lasts."

One night, I had a conversation with my father that helped me understand a concept I'd never really thought about.

He took a glass of plain water and asked me, "What is this?"

I said, "A glass of water."

Then he asked, "Is it pure or impure?"

"Pure," I replied, still confused.

He smiled. "This glass of water could be symbolic of truth. No matter how much you try to convince others you have a glass of impure water, eventually, they will see the truth, a glass of pure water."

Then he added, "But once you lie about the purity of your water, and someone asks for proof, what will you do?"

You're left with two options:

1. Add some impurities (dirt) to make the water match the lie.
2. Confess that you lied.

It's tempting to choose the first. But if you do, you not only make the glass impure, you corrupt your own heart too. We all make mistakes. It's human nature. So is asking for forgiveness. You want to live a value-based life? Then be mindful of the actions you take.

There are some mistakes we can't take back. For the rest, choose truth. Choose forgiveness.

I dwelled further on what he told me.

Sometimes, people choose to lie, not out of malice, but for the sake of others. Out of fear. Out of love. They hide parts of themselves, hoping to impress, to be accepted, or to avoid conflict. They avoid the things they love because someone else doesn't like them. They nod in agreement when their heart quietly disagrees. They silence their joy to keep the peace.

But this kind of lie… it doesn't set you free. It drains you.

And the saddest part?

The person you're doing it for starts believing that this version of you, the one hiding behind that filtered truth, is the real one. They get used to your mask. They build a relationship with your silence.

That's when I started thinking about people who forget to let others breathe.

And I wrote the following lines:

"There are many things you can give

if you're chasing a fleeting moment of happiness.

But if you want it to last,

give them freedom.

The freedom to be true to themselves."

So tell me, what's best to do?

Be true to yourself.

And let others do the same.

"Be careful about your actions, for your actions become your habits and your habits become your character."

Pause & Reflect

- When was the last time you pretended to be someone you're not, just to keep the peace?
- What would it feel like to show up as your full, honest self?
- Is there a truth you're afraid to speak, even to yourself?
- What belief about "pleasing others" do you want to release?
- What does being true to yourself look like in this season of life?

"Words, when used right,
Can heal any heart,
Connect with any soul,
Mend what's broken,
And gently guide the lost back to light."

Dear Reader,

If you've made it this far, I want you to take a breath and smile. You didn't just read a book, you showed up for yourself.

You took the time to reflect, to grow, to explore pieces of yourself that maybe you hadn't looked at in a while. And that? That's powerful.

You don't need to be perfect. You don't need to have it all figured out. You just need to keep showing up, with honesty, with grace, and with love for who you're becoming.

Your next chapter is already waiting for the real you to show up!

Now before you stuff your mind with the idea that it's not enough to be the way you are, let me share one last story with you.

One evening, I was on a call with an elderly lady. Our lives looked completely different.

I was surrounded; my mother, father, brothers, and kids filling my days. Every moment felt packed. Taking care of the kids, homeschooling my elder one, scribbling down thoughts before they slipped away, helping my mother, feeding little tummies, playing, reading from the pile of unfinished books. And in all of this, what I longed for most was time. Time to sit quietly. Time to process my thoughts. Time to move slower, without compromising my sleep.

But her? She was at home, all by herself. She had nothing but time. And yet, that was exactly what weighed heavy on her. She sighed and told me, "I don't know how I'll pass the time until morning."

She craved people, company, someone to care for. The very things I had but weren't appreciating enough. And she overlooked the gift of time she had.

Maybe this is our flaw as humans, always yearning for what we don't have, convincing ourselves life isn't enough.

But what if we paused? What if we reflected? Look at what we already hold in our hands?

What if we chose gratitude instead of longing?

Cherished life as it is, instead of chasing what it isn't?

Because maybe, just maybe, life is already enough.

Chase it, if you are sure you need it. And change it if something is unwanted in the bright future you're building. But don't miss what's already in your hand.

Sometimes, life is not about chasing the unknown.

But about a little pause.

The silent acknowledgment.

The whisper of gratitude.

For what you need is often

Already there for you.

And now, dear reader, I pass this truth to you: Your journey is yours alone. Grow at your pace. Pause when you need to. Celebrate often. And above all, live fully, in the way only you can and be grateful for it.

So *think, learn & flourish* — in your own way, in your own time!

With Love,

Neffi Rafiya